my time

5

SIMPLE STEPS
TO
FINANCIAL
FREEDOM

WIPE OUT DEBT AND BUILD WEALTH

DAN WILLIS

WHITAKER
HOUSE

Unless otherwise indicated, all Scripture quotations are taken from the King James Version of the Holy Bible. Scripture quotations marked (ESV) are taken from *The Holy Bible, English Standard Version*, © 2000, 2001, 1995 by Crossway Bibles, a division of Good News Publishers. Used by permission. All rights reserved. Scripture quotation marked (NIRV) is taken from the *Holy Bible, New International Reader's Version*®, NIRV®, © 1996, 1998 by Biblica. *All rights reserved throughout the world. Used by permission of Biblica.* Scripture quotations marked (NIV) are taken from the *Holy Bible, New International Version*®, NIV®, © 1973, 1978, 1984 by the International Bible Society. Used by permission of Zondervan. All rights reserved. Scripture quotations marked (NKJV) are taken from the *New King James Version*, © 1979, 1980, 1982, 1984 by Thomas Nelson, Inc. Used by permission. All rights reserved.

Boldface type in the Scripture quotations indicates the author's emphasis.

5 SIMPLE STEPS TO FINANCIAL FREEDOM:
Wipe Out Debt and Build Wealth

www.danwillis.org
www.thelighthousechurch.org
Twitter: http://twitter.com/PastorDanWillis
Facebook: http://facebook.com/lhcanations

ISBN: 978-1-64123-156-5
eBook ISBN: 978-1-64123-157-2
Printed in the United States of America
© 2019 by Dan Willis

Whitaker House
1030 Hunt Valley Circle
New Kensington, PA 15068
www.whitakerhouse.com

Library of Congress Cataloging-in-Publication Data (Pending)

No part of this book may be reproduced or transmitted in any form or by any means, electronic or mechanical—including photocopying, recording, or by any information storage and retrieval system—without permission in writing from the publisher. Please direct your inquiries to permissionseditor@whitakerhouse.com.

1 2 3 4 5 6 7 8 9 10 11 ⊔⊔ 26 25 24 23 22 21 20 19

CONTENTS

STEP 1:
STOP THE SPENDING

If I told you that you are only five steps away from wealth, what would you say to me? As a pastor and a shepherd, it really disturbs me that so many of God's people are struggling in financial situations. It hurts me because I've been in that situation more times than I want to remember. However, some years ago. God showed me and my wife, Linda, how to get out of debt and to be financially free. Now I'm on a mission to teach you how to do the same according to the Word of God.

MY STORY OF DEBT AND RESTORATION

I'm going to jump in right here with a personal confession. I'll be honest enough now to tell you what I wouldn't have been able tell you years ago. In my early years of ministry, I could not admit that I had twenty-three credit cards, and every one of them was maxed to the top. But it was for a good cause—we were building a church.

Lighthouse Church of All Nations has over five thousand members, but when I first started pastoring it at the age of sixteen, I only had sixteen members. In those days, the church needed many improvements. I've always been one who believes in giving God your best. Therefore, I decided that, to accomplish some of the things we were trying to do, it was best to do them first and to pay later. Nobody else would sign on the dotted line, so I used my credit cards to pay for carpeting. Then I charged speakers. I charged all kinds of things for that little storefront church, and I was so happy to do it because I was doing it for the Lord.

Now, I had easy access to credit cards because I had gotten applications in the mail when I was still in high school (which I thought was a blessing). I remember when Chase Bank sent me a $5,000 preapproval. I was shouting and telling everybody, "Look what the Lord has done!" It wasn't the Lord. It was the devil trying to take me under. The credit card companies didn't care that they were loading up some of us kids with so much debt that we were close to bankruptcy before we even graduated.

So here I was charging all these things to improve the ministry. But I couldn't sleep at night because I was getting in such financial bondage. Then one afternoon in a store as I went to charge something, I found myself saying under my breath, "In the name of Jesus, please let this card go through!"

The clerk looked up at me and said, "It was declined."

"Girl, something is wrong with your machine. You better swipe that card again!"

I knew full well that it wouldn't matter how many more times she swiped it, I had reached my limit. I could not charge one more thing. I had signed until I was denied. Every one of my cards was maxed. I finally realized that it made no sense to make ministry happen by running my credit card debt up and then paying it off at 19 percent interest. Now, don't get me wrong, not every penny on those cards came from stuff for the ministry. I bought some clothes. My wife bought some shoes. However, most of the charges on those cards were for the ministry.

I remember praying that night, "God, I'm trying to do all this for the ministry. Now my credit is jacked up, and I'm in a mess. And, God, it's all because of—."

I almost told God that it was because of Him that I was in this mess.

Boy, did the Holy Spirit get me. He said, "Nobody told you to do any of that."

"But God, if I hadn't charged for new carpet, nobody would have come to church."

"Folks aren't coming because of the carpet," God answered. "They're coming because they need a Word from the Lord."

That did something to me. It didn't matter to me anymore how I got in trouble. The only important thing was how to get out! So I told God, "All right, if You help me fix this, I will teach Your people how to do the same."

Today I can admit all of this to you because God gave me a plan from His Word that set me free. I have been debt-free from twenty-three credit cards for fifteen years. I owe no man anything but to love him.

I didn't get debt-free by draining the church or fleecing the congregation. I wasn't in the back room taking money from somebody. That's not my kind of gig. In fact, I haven't even taken a raise in over twenty years. I'm still living off what I was living on twenty years ago. My wife and I can do this because God gave me wisdom from His Word, and when we aligned ourselves with it. God provided for our needs through other ways. He opened doors of opportunity through television, music, and other things so we could build a church in Chicago. Thanks be to God, our brand-new church was constructed in 2015.

As I share with you the principles God gave me concerning faith and finances, I have no doubt in my mind that I heard from Him. This is not a "name it, claim it" or "blab it, grab it" theology. I promise that if you follow me as I follow Christ, what I am going to teach you from the Word of God will set you free financially in a way you never imagined. I don't say that with a question mark in my brain but with an exclamation point in my spirit!

> *This is not a "name it, claim it" or "blab it, grab it" theology. I promise that if you follow me as I follow Christ, what I am going to teach you from the Word of God will set you free financially in a way you never imagined.*

I'm not here to condemn you. I don't believe ... up" church; neither do I allow preachers with a repu... banging people in the head to get in the pulpit of Lighthou... I'm a shepherd who recognizes that everybody has had enough trauma in life. You don't need to come to church and experience trauma. You need deliverance and help when you come into the house of God.

I'm going to ask you now to strip away all your preconceived notions and presuppositions about money and finances. Do you know that, when God talks about your increase, He does not talk about it in terms of money? He talks about it in terms of riches and wealth. Many folks think wealth is far off. But I'm going to show you that, according to God's Word, there are just five steps between where you are now financially and being in a wealthy place.

THE DEBT-FREE SHREDDER

I issued a challenge to our congregation when I first taught on faith and finances. I said, "I'm going to get this party started. I have been waiting over a year to toss the final three credit cards that I have. I haven't used them in years." I pointed to two shredders sitting near the pulpit and told my members, "If you really want to get debt-free and you've got credit cards in your pocket or purse, why are you hanging on to them?"

What if we hung on to Jesus the same way we hang on to our Visa cards? I'm just saying. We claim to need the credit cards in case of emergencies. But you've got Lane Bryant, Payless Shoes,

Sears, J. C. Penney, Carson's, and Macy's cards. Really? All those are for emergencies?

The three credit cards that I still had at the time had zero balances. I turned on the shredder, put one of my cards in it, and said, "This is the sound of me getting debt-free. I'm going to shred one of my cards at each of the three services I preach today. And I hope we'll hear other people getting debt-free. While I'm teaching, get your credit cards out of your wallet. I don't care if you're shaking; I'll help you stand up when you get down here."

The first person to come was a woman in our congregation. She hesitated when she got in front of the shredder.

"Is that card maxed?" I asked.

She nodded.

"Listen, kids, if they're maxed, you can't use them anyway! They're worthless. And all you're doing is paying $14 a month on a $2,000 balance. It will take you eight years to pay that off. Put it in this shredder."

She was shaking. Her forehead was sweating. "No, I can't do it," she moaned.

"You'll be all right," I told her. "Trust me. I've been where you are."

She found the strength to shred her cards, and more people came forward to follow her lead. Some of them seemed relieved. Others were visibly apprehensive. To lighten the mood, I said, "Don't say you don't want to walk up here because you don't have the right shoes on today. The devil is a liar! Come up here and put your credit cards in this shredder. The first people who are going to be set free are the people who just came down to put their credit cards in here. You're going to hear their praise reports soon."

Nearly two hundred credit cards were shredded during those three services.

FAITH AND FINANCES

It may sound like I'm a prosperity teacher, but here's my spin on prosperity: if you walk with Jesus and do what Matthew 6:33 (ESV) says, you *"seek first the kingdom of God and his righteousness, and all things will be added to you."* Everything you need to prosper, God wants to give to you. He said, *"It is [His] good pleasure to give you the kingdom"* (Luke 12:32 ESV). God is not trying to bankrupt you. He is not trying to hold you hostage in your finances. God wants you to be set free not only in your finances but also in your faith.

You see, faith and finances are spiritually attracted to each other. Not attached to each other but attracted to each other. If they were attached to each other, everyone walking in faith would automatically have finances. Some Christians of great faith believe that not having money is more godly than having money. So they neither desire nor have money. I don't judge them, but I know what the Bible says. *"The love of money is the root of all evil"* (1 Timothy 6:10). It doesn't say that money is the root of evil. God's not mad if you possess money. He's only displeased when you allow your money to possess you. God wants us to prosper.

> *Beloved, I wish above all things* [or "I hope above all things" or "I have faith above everything else"] *that thou mayest prosper.*   (3 John 1:2)

Remember when they put the candles on your last birthday cake? What did they tell you to do? Make a wish. A wish is something that you're hoping for, longing for, or believing in faith for. Third John 2 says, *"Beloved, I wish* [or "I hope" or "I have faith"] *that thou mayest prosper."* That's why I say that faith and finances work in tandem. If you have finances, you can always tie it back to faith somewhere in your life. Each one affects the other. You cannot have faith without your finances being affected, and you will not have finances without your faith being increased. Faith and finances attract each other. They call for each other. They woo each other. People walking by faith attract finances.

> *Faith and finances work in tandem.*
> *If you have finances, you can always tie it back to faith*
> *somewhere in your life. Each one affects the other.*
> *You cannot have faith without your finances*
> *being affected, and you will not have finances*
> *without your faith being increased.*

Most of us who are broke and in financial trouble are numb to faith. Stress from constant calls about our delinquent credit depletes our faith. You might want to rejoice and praise God under those circumstances, but let's face it, it's difficult to be a man or woman of faith when your finances are a wreck. However, if you can learn how to flip the script on the devil and let your faith rise, I guarantee you that your finances will release.

As you take this journey to financial freedom, your authority and source of wisdom must be God's Word, not the traditional denomination you were raised in that didn't talk about faith. Not your mama. Not your auntie. Not the priest, the nun, the rabbi, or the old preacher man. Not even your ex-husband. Many things they said about finances were wrong. When I hung out with broke people, I spent more money, because hopelessness gives you a pseudo-license to overspend. When I started hanging with successful people, I started talking about freedom from debt. Proverbs 18:21 shares, *"Death and life are in the power of the tongue"*! I became desirous of being debt-free! One of my assistants said, "The possibility becomes a reality once you hear people around you speak about being debt-free!"

God's Word is the source of wisdom because the Word works. It accomplishes what it has been sent to do. The Bible states that it's impossible for God's Word to go out and to return void. (See Isaiah 55:11.) If the spoken rhema, or Word, of God is sent (confessed) over your circumstances, it must come back and yield a harvest. You might be lying flat on your back with a respirator tube down your throat. Meditate on Isaiah 53:5: *"With his stripes we are healed."* Know that when His Word is sent, it comes back with a result.

Trust God's Word as the authority as you seek to get out of debt. Don't take financial advice from people who are broke. I've been on a diet since I was in my mother's womb (well, maybe not quite that long). But I learned not to take advice from folks who have not been able to manage their own weight. On the other hand, if somebody tells me they lost twenty-five pounds, the first thing I say is, "How did you do it?" It's the same when it comes to credit. Don't let someone who is bankrupt give you financial advice. Stick with the Word of God. It says so much about this subject. Let's start with this:

> For the LORD thy God blesseth thee, as he promised thee: and thou shalt lend unto many nations, but thou shalt not borrow.   (Deuteronomy 15:6)

Someone is saying, "Wait, I'm not supposed to be borrowing?" It is a commandment from God that you're not supposed to be in debt. Nowadays, debt seems to be the modern way. But we're Christians before we're Americans. We believe the Word of God first, and the Word says we're not supposed to borrow. Shred that credit card application you have in your stack of mail at home. If you've lived without that card this long, you don't need it. The temporary pleasure you'd get from it would be completely overshadowed by the result—servitude.

> The rich ruleth over the poor, and the borrower is servant to the lender.   (Proverbs 22:7)

> The rich rule over the poor, and the borrower is slave to the lender.   (Proverbs 22:7 NIV)

I saw a televangelist who used that verse to say that debt is a sin. The Bible doesn't teach that. Debt is not a sin. You will not go to hell for debt. What the Bible does teach is that debt puts you in bondage. You walk the floor at night while your creditors are sleeping. Still want to defend holding on to your credit cards? Think on this:

The blessing of the LORD, it maketh rich, and he addeth no sorrow with it.   (Proverbs 10:22)

If that credit card was such a good thing, you wouldn't have so much sorrow over it, would you? God's plan is not for you to have sleepless nights because you can't pay your bills. Hear His kingdom plan for us:

Beloved, I wish above all things that thou mayest prosper and be in health, even as thy soul prospereth. (3 John 1:2)

But seek ye first the kingdom of God, and his righteousness; and all these things shall be added unto you.
(Matthew 6:33)

Owe no man any thing but to love one another: for he that loveth another hath fulfilled the law.   (Romans 13:8)

Here's the problem: We want to receive the parts of God's kingdom plan that say, "I wish you would prosper" and "It's my good pleasure to give you the kingdom." But we turn a deaf ear when God warns against being in debt. We want to have our credit cards, our equity loans, and all this lending going on, and then we wonder why we come to church and can't feel the presence of God. Stress over our lack of finances has annihilated our faith.

BREAKING THE CYCLE OF DEBT

Something has to break. We have to crush that debt cycle and shift out of the mentality of "I want it, so I'm going to get it." If you can't pay for it, you shouldn't get it. It's as simple as that.

I know that's not always easy. How many have been accosted by that lady in stretch pants and blood-red lipstick at a department store? You know that's a hot mess. She blocks your path and says, "Would you like to sign up for a credit card?"

She's basically saying, "Let me help you put yourself in debt." And when you don't fall for it, she adds, "You'll get fifteen percent off on your first purchase if you sign up for a card." She left out that your monthly payments will have 20 percent interest tacked on to them. No, I don't want to sign up for a credit card! I am delivered from that stuff.

So many things work against us when we're in bondage to debt. The *Chicago Sun-Times* once did an article about NSF charges. A lot of us know what NSF stands for: nonsufficient funds, not enough money, not sufficient stuff. However you say it, it means you wrote the check and did not have enough money in the bank to cover it.

Banks make so much money off NSF fees. They charge as much as thirty-nine dollars for one bounced check. Now let me take you to school. Three NSF charges in a month add up to enough to pay off a building fund pledge for one hundred dollars. See how being a slave to debt makes us unable to bless the kingdom? It's not that we don't have the money. It's that it's tied up in debt.

That newspaper article got me thinking about how much money we pay in interest and fees on money that we borrow. I decided to research payday loan centers. I've never been to any, but I called one and asked what the repayment terms would be if I qualified for a loan for five hundred dollars.

In a friendly and energetic voice, the lady told me the interest rate, said I would have six months to pay it back, and that there would be a penalty if I paid it off early.

I had a calculator sitting right on my desk and added everything up as she talked. Barely able to contain my shock, I said, "Ma'am, hold up. I'm only borrowing five hundred dollars, but with the terms you just gave me, I will have paid back more than two thousand dollars at the end of six months!"

All of a sudden, her good nature changed. She said in a sour voice, "Do you want the loan or not?"

I said, "No, I do not! In fact, I'm going to preach against you Sunday at church, in Jesus's name."

After I hung up, I started googling to find out where the payday loan stores were located. There was not one in the nice suburbs of Chicago. But as I searched the West Side of Chicago, there were twelve payday loan stores in a two-mile area. These companies have targeted people who are already in financial bondage. You tell me that's not Egypt keeping you in slavery to pharaoh and this world's system.

> *God wants you to be free, but we're not really convicted about being in debt. Do you realize that being in debt is a spiritual condition, not a financial condition? It is a sign that greed has set in.*

When some of you say, "Pastor Dan, I can't give to the church," I know you can't, because you're paying 400 percent interest on payday loans.

God wants you to be free, but we're not really convicted about being in debt. Do you realize that being in debt is a spiritual condition, not a financial condition? It is a sign that greed has set in. Rather than live with the things you've got, you have to have more and more. But the Bible says,

> *Keep your lives free from the love of money and be content with what you have, because God has said, "Never will I leave you; never will I forsake you."*   (Hebrews 13:5 NIV)

I'll never forget waking up on my sixteenth birthday and getting so upset because I didn't get a Lincoln Continental. True story. From the age of fourteen, I had told my parents I wanted a Lincoln Continental. Now, what was I going to do with a Lincoln Continental at age sixteen? I wanted the bling of owning that car. The day I turned sixteen, I jumped out of bed and went outside. No Lincoln Continental. I ran to my mother and asked, "Where did you park it?"

She said, "I've got six children. How am I supposed to get you a Lincoln Continental?"

Cars are irrelevant to me today. After having four kids of my own while simultaneously going to college and working a couple of jobs, I learned that it didn't make a difference what car I drove. I had a Volvo, and I had to put a cardboard floorboard in the back to keep my kids from scraping their feet on the pavement as I drove. It didn't matter to me what people thought. I'd walk by that Volvo and say, "That's all right. She's paid for!"

God had to teach me to get over myself. But some of us still insist on having the latest bling. We want the iPhone, the iPad, and everything else. Now mind you, we can't pay our bills, but we've got to have the latest. I learned that just because you have stuff doesn't mean you have money. Stuff is often a sign of pain and heartache. To relieve it, some of us eat our way through it. Some of us shop our way through it. We think that food or shopping will not take our pain away. Nothing can take your pain away but the blood of Jesus Christ. He's able!

> *Debt is especially dangerous when we are tempted to rob God (our primary Creditor) to pay people (our secondary creditors).*

Debt is especially dangerous when we are tempted to rob God (our primary Creditor) to pay people (our secondary creditors). Who gave you life this morning? Who gave you breath in your body? Who gave you health? Who gave you strength? Who woke you up this morning? So to whom do you owe the most? God.

One thing Linda and I never compromised on while we were becoming debt-free was our seed-giving to the Lord. God says,

> *Will a man rob God? Yet you have robbed Me! But you say, "In what way have we robbed You?" In tithes and offerings. You are cursed with a curse.*   (Malachi 3:8–9 NKJV)

You're under a curse if you are robbing God. It took me a minute to understand this because I used to feel sorry for people who were broke all the time. But then I got the revelation that if they don't tithe, they are supposed to be broke. If you rob God,

He says, "You're going to miss out on something I wanted to give you." But look at what God says He's going to do if you tithe:

> "Bring the whole tithe into the storehouse, that there may be food in my house. Test me in this," says the LORD Almighty, "and see if I will not throw open the floodgates of heaven and pour out so much blessing that there will not be room enough to store it. I will prevent pests from devouring your crops, and the vines in your fields will not drop their fruit before it is ripe," says the LORD Almighty. "Then all the nations will call you blessed, for yours will be a delightful land," says the LORD Almighty.   (Malachi 3:10–12 NIV)

This brings us back to the conviction that debt is a serious spiritual condition. I'm sure you'd like people to look at you and think, "Boy, he's got it together. He has plenty of money. He doesn't owe anybody anything." God's Word just gave you the formula for it, and holding back money from Him is never part of the solution. It is a source of financial downfall. It's this simple: your position in giving always determines your position in living. If you give third class, you'll live third class. If you give first-class, you'll live first-class because favor chased you down.

You say you can't give to God because you're in a financial bind. You can't afford *not* to give to God if you're serious about getting out of that situation. I have living proof of that. A husband and wife in our leadership team sent me an email just before I taught a series on faith and finances to my congregation. It read:

> Pastor, I got so excited when you announced you were going to teach on faith and finances. I know for a fact

it works. You know we never tell any of our business, but I knew the time would come for us to tell what God did for us. Two thousand five was the worst year we ever had. A lady stole so much money from our business that I almost got bitter. But we stayed focused.

It took us three years to figure our way out. We lost everything, but we kept tithing, giving, coming to church, and working in ministry. This is very hard to do when you're under serious financial pressure. Some of our own family members told us that we were failures and would never succeed.

In 2008, things began to look up. We started building a home. After nine months, the home was completed. We were excited. But when we got ready to close, something appeared on our credit. The builders still let us move in, but they put us in a lease agreement until our credit got straight. I was so disappointed. We felt like we were back to square one. But we kept on believing and tithing.

In March of 2009, our credit had improved, and we were ready to buy the house. But the builder got greedy and didn't want to sell it to us at a price we could afford. So we broke our lease agreement in May of 2009, not sure where we would go. We still kept the faith, though.

One Sunday after church, we stopped by a subdivision. They had some nice houses we were interested in. The builder's representative called me that Monday and told me that if I could get over to the subdivision, he had something to show me. When I got there, he showed me a model house. It was beautiful. But I was thinking, *We can't afford this.*

He told me that the builder was going bankrupt and needed to sell it immediately. The model came with appliances, window treatments, and every room fully furnished. Then he quoted the price. Pastor, it was twenty thousand dollars less than what the bank had qualified us for. We were under budget. There was a waiting list for the house. But the man said, "When I met you and your husband on Sunday, there was something different about you guys. If you want this house, it's yours."

Three weeks ago, we closed on that house. We moved in, and the only thing we took in there was our clothing. We are still in shock. Pastor, we had to go through everything we went through so God would bless us and we would remain humble. But I know for sure that tithes and offering, together with being in consistent covenant with Lighthouse and God, made it possible. God gets the glory!

That's the favor of God. When you do right by God, God does right by you. This couple's great faith attracted a financial blessing beyond their wildest imagination.

CREATING A DEBT-FREE LEGACY

I once had a revelation about faith and finances while preaching at a funeral for a ninety-four-year-old woman. Someone from her family got up and said, "The most beautiful thing about her was that she paid all her bills on time. She was never late." They were so happy about that. It might sound like something odd to say at a funeral, but it got me to thinking.

A year before that, I had buried my precious ninety-five-year-old grandmother, who had been the same way. She'd never had a credit card. She hadn't even had a checking account. My mother is now eighty-something years old, and she's never had any credit cards either. These are three women of great faith. Miracles, signs, and wonders flowed through them.

The Spirit of God reminded me of two other people of great faith who never used credit cards: Oral Roberts and R. W. Schambach. Richard Roberts, my good friend and the son of Oral Roberts, once told me that his father, who was in his nineties at the time, had never had a credit card. I used to listen to R. W. Schambach on the radio stating that he didn't have any credit cards either. But under these men's ministries, blinded eyes were opened and lame legs were healed. Why? Because they didn't walk in debt. These men and women walked by faith and not by sight (see 2 Corinthians 5:7), depending totally on God and not once looking to Visa or MasterCard to meet their needs. God's power was free to flow through them because the spirit of debt had no power to block their faith.

However, we have credit cards maxed to the top and no miracles flowing through us. Your grandparents didn't live by all that credit card nonsense. If they couldn't afford it, they didn't buy it. You'd be the same way right now if you didn't have credit cards to fall back on. Have you ever noticed how stingy you tend to be when you're walking through the mall with a hundred dollars in your pocket but no credit card? You catch sight of those shoes you thought you couldn't live without, but you just can't make yourself part with that hundred-dollar bill. You walk right on by those shoes, saying, "I'll just keep the ones I have on." But credit cards have put us in bondage and slavery. We just whip them out, charge merchandise, and pay up to 49.9 percent interest.

> *God has plans, dreams, and visions for your life.*
> *You're supposed to be sowing into the kingdom of God*
> *to get the work accomplished, to get the church built,*
> *and to do all the things God wants.*

God has plans, dreams, and visions for your life. You're supposed to be sowing into the kingdom of God to get the work accomplished, to get the church built, and to do all the things God wants. What if He told you to plant a seed to send a missionary with the gospel to a foreign land? With all my heart, I believe that any Christian who makes an effort to come to church wants to listen to God and to please Him. You wouldn't get up early on a Sunday morning and go to church if you didn't. But we have constricted and restricted ourselves so much that when the Holy Spirit moves, we're scared to death to step out on faith.

We're living above our means. Every month, we're just deferring debt. The only way to get out of debt is to start living below your means. If you make $2,000 a month, learn how to live on $1,800. You're going to have to cut the credit cards up and learn how to deny yourself. And you're going to have to learn how to cook at home. The stores still sell a three pack of ramen noodles for a dollar. You might have to commit to eating them until you get out of debt.

Credit cards enabled you to buy more than you could afford. Discarding them will force you to curb your spending. When God walked me through the process of eliminating my debt, He first had me cut up the credit cards and stop spending. I challenge you to step out in faith and make that sacrifice.

In the Bible, every sacrifice came with an offering. I encourage you to sow a seed in the kingdom of God. I'm not talking about tithes and offering but a sacrificial seed for a special harvest.

I know from my personal experience that if you shred your credit cards and stop spending, you will experience some ups and downs. Your faith level will begin to go up, while your burden of debt will begin to go down.

PRAYER

Heavenly Father, I come before You today, submitting my finances to You. Thank You for guiding me with the wisdom and knowledge to make decisions that will lead me to being debt free. Thank You for self-control with spending, favor with creditors, and reliance on You as my source of all things. I love You, Lord, and I make the choice today to begin honoring You with my finances. In Jesus's name, amen.

2

STEP 2:
BUDGETING IS COOL

"A *merry heart doeth good like a medicine*" (Proverbs 17:22), so I want to share a little humor as we get into this chapter on budgeting.

Buddy and his wife, Edna, went to the state fair every year, and every year, Buddy would say, "Edna, I'd like to ride in that helicopter."

Edna always replied, "I know, Buddy. But that helicopter ride costs fifty dollars. You know we're on a budget, and fifty bucks is fifty bucks!"

One year, Buddy and Edna went to the fair, and he said, "Edna, listen, honey. I'm eighty-five years old. If I don't take that helicopter ride today, I might never get the chance."

To this, Edna replied, "Buddy, that helicopter ride costs fifty dollars. We're on a budget, and fifty bucks is fifty bucks!"

The pilot overheard the couple and said, "Folks, I'll make you a deal. I'll take both of you up for a ride in my helicopter, and if you can stay completely quiet for the entire ride, I won't charge you a penny. But if you say one word, you owe me fifty dollars."

Old Buddy and Edna agreed, and away they went up in the helicopter. The pilot did all kinds of crazy maneuvers and daredevil tricks, but he couldn't elicit one peep out of the old couple. When they landed, the pilot said over his shoulder, "Wow, I am impressed, old man. No matter what I did, neither one of you said a word."

Buddy replied from the back seat of the plane, "To tell you the truth, I almost said something when Edna fell out. But we're on a budget, and fifty bucks is fifty bucks!"

Of course, this is fiction, but it serves most of us well to take such a hard line where our budget is concerned because credit card debt will take you to hell. Not literally, but it will make you curse. It will make you sick. It will make you hate people.

That's not God's will for you. I'm tired of God's people walking the floor at night, worrying about finances while the devil is sleeping. It ought to be that tonight you go to sleep and make the devil wonder what to do with you. Your faith should rise until the devil doesn't know how to handle you any longer. That is your birthright. That is your promise.

And it shall come to pass, if thou shalt hearken diligently unto the voice of the LORD thy God, to observe and to do all his commandments which I command thee this day, that the LORD thy God will set thee on high above all nations of the earth: and all these blessings shall come on thee, and overtake thee, if thou shalt hearken unto the voice of the LORD *thy God. Blessed shalt thou be in the city, and blessed shalt thou be in the field. Blessed shall be the fruit of thy body, and the fruit of thy ground, and the fruit of thy cattle, the increase of thy kine [cattle], and the flocks of thy sheep. Blessed shall be thy basket and thy store. Blessed shalt thou be when thou comest in, and blessed shalt thou be when thou goest out. The* LORD *shall cause thine enemies that rise up against thee to be smitten before thy face: they shall come out against thee one way, and flee before thee seven ways. The* LORD *shall command the blessing upon thee in thy storehouses, and in all that thou settest thine hand unto; and he shall bless thee in the land which the* LORD *thy God giveth thee. The* LORD *shall establish thee an holy people unto himself, as he hath sworn unto thee, if thou shalt keep the commandments of the* LORD *thy God, and walk in his ways. And all people of the earth shall see that thou art called by the name of the* LORD*; and they shall be afraid of thee. And the* LORD *shall make thee plenteous in goods, in the fruit of thy body, and in the fruit of thy cattle, and in the fruit of thy ground, in the land which the* LORD *sware unto thy fathers to give thee. The* LORD *shall open unto thee his good treasure, the heaven to give the rain unto thy land in his season, and to bless all the work of thine hand: and thou shalt lend unto many nations, and thou shalt not borrow. And the* LORD *shall make thee the head, and not the tail; and thou shalt be above only, and thou shalt not be beneath; if that thou hearken unto the commandments of the* LORD *thy God, which I command thee* *this day, to observe and to do them.*

(Deuteronomy 28:1–13)

This is a promise from the Word of God to the seed of Abraham, which you are part of. All these blessings will roll up on you and overtake you if you hearken to the voice of the Lord your God. Did you notice that this is a two-sided coin? There's God's part, and there's your part. You can never do God's part, and God will never do your part. Your part is to walk in obedience to the Word of God. With that in mind, this is the objective I want to teach you: be debt-free at all costs.

After I drew a line in the sand and said, "I'm getting rid of my credit cards. Debt stops today," my next step was to commit to a godly, prioritized budget. God honors His principles. In other words, if you do your part, God will do His. I understand that getting on a budget is scary; when Linda and I first got on a budget, I was terrified. But the Word of God is where I found my security. You'll be all right on a budget. You can do this. God has got your back, and He is an absolutely awesome God.

Who has measured the waters in the hollow of his hand, or with the breadth of his hand marked off the heavens? Who has held the dust of the earth in a basket, or weighed the mountains on the scales and the hills in a balance?

(Isaiah 40:12 NIV)

Surely the nations are like a drop in a bucket; they are regarded as dust on the scales; he weighs the islands as though they were fine dust.   (Isaiah 40:15 NIV)

Even to your old age and gray hairs I am he, I am he who will sustain you. I have made you and I will carry you; I will sustain you and I will rescue you.   (Isaiah 46:4 NIV)

God has His part down. He will bring you through your current situation, even in the face of statistics that say that 68 percent of Americans are so in debt that they have no idea how they will ever get out of it.[1] But you have to do your part, which includes seeking first the kingdom of God (see Matthew 6:33), as well as bringing all the tithes into the storehouse (see Malachi 3:10). I'm putting your feet to the fire. You're going to have to count the cost.

For which of you, intending to build a tower, sitteth not down first, and counteth the cost, whether he have sufficient to finish it? Lest haply, after he hath laid the foundation, and is not able to finish it, all that behold it begin to mock him.   (Luke 14:28–29)

THE B-WORD

The Bible asks, "What man fails to count the cost of an endeavor?" Budgeting is a means of accountability, a way to count the cost. We go broke because we have no budget, and we have no budget because we have no discipline. We have no discipline because we can't stick with anything for long. We give up on everything—marriages, churches, friendships, and dreams. Some of you are going to die with a dream still in you because

---

1. Jade Scipioni, "68% of Americans in debt doubt they'll ever pay it off," Fox Business, January 11, 2018 https://www.foxbusiness.com/markets/68-of-americans-in-debt-doubt-theyll-ever-pay-it-off (accessed October 11, 2018).

somebody told you that you couldn't. We give up over any shred of an excuse.

> *We go broke because we have no budget, and we have no budget because we have no discipline.*
> *We have no discipline because we can't stick with anything for long. We give up on everything— marriages, churches, friendships, and dreams.*

We ought to be entrepreneurs, recording artists, or whatever we dream to be, but somebody told us the economy is too bad to try. God is not bound by the world's economy. He said that He knows how to make streams in the desert, satisfy your soul in a drought, make you like a watered garden, and make you fruitful. (See Isaiah 58:11.) Didn't He know how to take care of Noah in a flood? Didn't He know how to take care of Elijah and Elisha? Doesn't God know how to clothe the lilies of the field? (See Matthew 6:28.) Take no thought for your life. If God knows how to do those things, He's got you in the midst of your economic drought. When everything else is going down, that's the prime opportunity for people with godly insight and wisdom to gain wealth. Why can't we do that? Because we have no discipline.

Almost everybody has had a budget at some point in his or her life and has said it didn't work. It's not that it didn't work. It's that he or she didn't work it. It goes right back to the spiritual problem.

He that hath no rule over his own spirit is like a city that is
broken down, and without walls.   (Proverbs 25:28)

We've learned how to go to church, beat the tambourine, shout, speak in tongues, fall out, and scream and holler. But we are bankrupt because we don't commit to keeping to our budget. It doesn't make any sense. It is time for God's people to learn to walk in accordance with the Word of God. Most of us could be debt-free quicker than you would believe.

> *It is time for God's people to learn to walk in accordance with the Word of God. Most of us could be debt-free quicker than you would believe.*

THE BUDGET MATRIX

I'm issuing a challenge for you to fill out the budget matrix on pages 34–35 and religiously stick to it for thirty days, come hell or high water. It's very simple. First, write down your income. Then write down your tithe (a tenth of your earnings). Make sure to put your tithe in there because I can't help you if you don't want to obey God's Word. The Bible says, *"Bring ye all the tithes into the storehouse"* (Malachi 3:10). Next, itemize all of your expenses. Be specific and honest with this. You can't improve your financial situation if you are unaware of how much is coming in and how much is going out.

The final box on the budget matrix is your 5 percent overage amount. Your goal is for there to be an overage—money left over

BUDGETING CHART

INCOME	
Salary 1	
Salary 2	
Bonuses	
Misc. Income	
TOTAL INCOME	

EXPENSES			
TITHES & OFFERING		**PETS**	
Tithes		Food	
Offering		Medical	
Charity		Grooming / Other	
HOUSE		**INSURANCE**	
Mortgage / Rent		Home	
Phone		Health	
Electricity		Life	
Gas		Other	
Water & Sewer		**PERSONAL**	
Cable & Internet		Medical	
Waste Removal		Hair / Nails	
AUTOMOBILES		Clothing	
Auto Loan Payment		Dry Cleaning	
Bus / Taxi / Uber Fare		Gym	
Insurance		Other	
Licensing & Fees			
Fuel			
Maintenance			

EXPENSES			
FOOD		**ENTERTAINMENT**	
Groceries		Movies	
Dining Out/Fast Food		Concerts	
OTHER LOANS		Sporting Events	
Student Loans		Theater	
Credit Card		Other	
Credit Card		**SAVINGS**	
Credit Card		Roth IRA	
		Vacation Savings	
		Other	
		TOTAL EXPENSE	
	Total Income -Total Expense		
		Difference	
		Overage-5% of Income	

when you subtract expenses from income. Ideally, that overage should equal 5 percent of your income. Put that amount in the box, whatever it is—even if it is not currently being reached. The plan is for you to have that amount left over at the end of each month, even after you've paid your tithe and everything in your budget.

The idols in our lives keep us from having a budget. "Pastor Dan, I don't have any idols. I'm saved, sanctified, and filled with the Holy Spirit." No, you do have idols. Why else would you pay $4.95 for one cup of coffee at Starbucks, then go to church and give God $2.00? You can walk through the mall and buy a $300 gold chain you hadn't planned on buying, but if the Holy Spirit said to give a $300 offering, you'd retort, "Holler at your boy, God!" You eat out twice a week, perhaps $20 each time. With your $5 tip both times, it totals $50 a week. That's $200 a month. You are spending $2,600 a year eating crab legs dipped in butter, while the world is going to hell.

Let's go back to the Word to see what it says about budgeting.

I went by the field of the slothful, and by the vineyard of the man void of understanding; and, lo, it was all grown over with thorns, and nettles had covered the face thereof, and the stone wall thereof was broken down. Then I saw, and considered it well: I looked upon it, and received instruction. Yet a little sleep, a little slumber, a little folding of the hands to sleep: so shall thy poverty come as one that travelleth; and thy want as an armed man. (Proverbs 24:30–34)

I was out of town one week when one of my kids called me and said, "Dad, I just woke up."

"Just woke up? It's one-thirty in the afternoon."

He yawned and said, "Yeah, I know. Where can I get ten dollars to go eat?"

I said, "Son, today you're fasting!" I wasn't playing. The Bible says the man who doesn't work doesn't eat. (See 2 Thessalonians 3:10.) If I don't teach my children that they can't expect to have their needs met while sleeping their lives away, they will become like the slothful man in Proverbs 24. I'm not going to be out here singing, preaching, and busting my tail while he sleeps half a day.

That's why some of you need to put your baby daddy out. You're the only one working. He hasn't had a job in six months, but you're buying Nike shoes and Heineken for him. Put him out. I'm not talking about putting your husband out. I'm talking about your boyfriend, who has never proposed to you. He says, "What's a piece of paper? We don't need no paper." He doesn't need a bed to sleep in!

Break the cycle. We're the seed of Abraham.

> If you belong to Christ, then you are Abraham's seed, and heirs according to the promise.   (Galatians 3:29 NIV)

Do you remember what Deuteronomy 28 says? You are heirs of those promises. Blessed shall you be going in. Blessed shall you be coming out. Blessed shall be the fruit of your womb. Everything you put your hand to shall prosper.

God gives us all these blessings, and we never enjoy them. We must be disciplined; otherwise, we'll pass our poor habits on to the next generation. Over the years, I've watched people who are late for church. Now I'm pastoring their grown kids, who are also late for church. I watched parents in the church who have an issue with tithing. Guess what? Their kids have an issue with tithing, too. These are generational curses. We duplicate what our parents did. When parents live with no budget and do not get their finances together, their kids and grandkids end up having a hard time understanding the importance of budgeting.

You have to break that cycle. It doesn't matter if your parents chose not to live according to the Word of God. Continue to love them but break the cycle. As for me and my house, we're going to serve the Lord. (See Joshua 24:15.) Maybe they never saw the value of tithing. But as for me and my house, we're going to be debt-free. We're not going to live in poverty. We're going to do it God's way.

You need a budget now. Don't wait until after God brings you through. Perhaps you're still telling yourself that you can't keep a budget because you've failed so many times before. God is faithful. If you do your part, He will do His.

No matter how far you've traveled down the wrong road, the only solution is to turn back. "Pastor Dan, I'm going to get a budget together someday." Do it today. You need a budget now. Don't wait until after God brings you through. Perhaps you're still telling yourself that you can't keep a budget because you've failed so many times before. God is faithful. If you do your part, He will do His. When Israel went to the Jordan River, the Red Sea, and any place where they could not see a way out, divine miracles from God got them where they needed to go. And the first thing they did when God brought deliverance and they came through a dilemma was to lay a seed on the altar.

Some of you are at an impossible river today. But today's test will be tomorrow's testimony when you get on the other side. Follow me as I follow Christ. Sow a seed into the kingdom of God for debt elimination.

Even though we're discussing faith and finances, you can still find Jesus. It depends on how your heart is. If you need a change in your life and are ready to follow Jesus, repeat the following prayer.

PRAYER

Heavenly Father, You are the Creator and Source of all things. Everything I have is Yours. Help me to be a wise steward of all that You have entrusted me with on earth, including my finances. I desire to make better choices with my money. Help me to learn to trust You. Help me to put You first by tithing 10 percent of my income to my local church to further the gospel. I trust Your Word that You will open the windows of heaven so that I can continue to be a blessing to those around me. In Jesus's name, amen.

3

STEP 3:
THE PAYOFF PLAN

Gods Word tells us that we're to be good stewards of what He has given us. We should desire to have integrity in the way we manage what He has blessed us with. That's why I'm going to teach you the actual process of paying off all your debt.

You must come at this with a firm resolve that the purpose of getting out of debt is to stay out of debt. You're not supposed to shred your credit cards, then instantly turn around and apply for more. Neither are you supposed to pay all your credit cards off to just run the balances back up once more. You should never want to go back to that way of living again. Your testimony should be that you fell down but you got back up. Psalm 119:67 says,

Before I was afflicted I went astray: but now have I kept thy word.

Of course, you're not happy about what you've had to go through financially. But the Bible says it's good that you've been afflicted because then you'll be willing for somebody to teach you. (See Psalm 119:71.)

ATTITUDE ADJUSTMENT

First, let me teach you about the attitude you must have if you want to eliminate debt. That attitude is this: Don't be a victim. News flash—you created the situation, so get the right attitude. It is not "Woe is me," "Everybody's against me," "If you hadn't given me this credit card, I wouldn't be in debt." Nobody held a gun to my head and made me sign until I was denied. I did it. Take responsibility for the decisions you made that got you in trouble. Don't be a victim.

Let me teach you about the attitude you must have if you want to eliminate debt. That attitude is this: Don't be a victim. News flash—you created the situation, so get the right attitude. Take responsibility for the decisions you made that got you in trouble.

PROACTIVE COMMUNICATION

After you've had an attitude adjustment, you need to learn how to communicate proactively and positively with lenders. When I had all those credit cards, the collectors called and called. According to Deuteronomy 28, blessings were supposed to be chasing me down, but instead, credit collectors were chasing me down. Most of the time when they called, I was "unavailable." I'd see their number, and I'd tell my wife, "Say I'm not here." Then I'd run out the back door so she wouldn't be lying about it. Whenever I took their call, I'd get on the defensive in a hurry. "Why are you calling me? The law says you can't harass people." I didn't know the first thing about the law.

One day God said to me, "Call your lenders proactively. They've been chasing you. Now you chase them."

I got a piece of paper and wrote down the name and phone number of each credit card company, as well as how much I owed for each card.

God said, "Call them all. You're behind with every one of them. Call them proactively and see what you can work out with them. But tell them in a positive voice because your attitude has changed." Even though you're in debt, God is honored when you do the right thing.

So I started calling them. I was kind of shaky on the first couple of calls, but by the time I got to the eighteenth one, I was an expert. Somewhere along the line, I remember talking with one credit collector. When she answered the phone, I said, "Hi, my name is Pastor Dan, and I'm calling to talk about my account."

"What's your account number?" she asked dryly.

I gave her my account number and said, "Isn't this a beautiful day? The sun is shining."

She said, "Sir, what do you want?"

She was so used to dealing with rudeness and inflammatory conversations that she was in the mode to be attacked. I wondered to myself what it must be like to get up, go to work, and expect to be attacked. She was just doing her job.

So I said to her, "You've been calling and calling me, and I haven't been available. But today I'm calling you because God has been telling me that He is honored by good stewardship." I didn't know if she was an atheist or a believer, but God had told me to come clean with all of them and tell them that it was a spiritual condition I was in and that I would be honoring Him if I made good on the debts I owed.

> *God had told me to come clean with all of my debtors*
> *and tell them that it was a spiritual condition*
> *I was in and that I would be honoring Him*
> *if I made good on the debts I owed.*

I asked, "Would you cut my interest rate or lower my balance?" I had asked the same of all the creditors I had called. One-third of them either lowered my interest rate or my balance. I found that, as jacked up as my finances were, they were willing to work with me because I called them with the right attitude.

I remember that conversation ending like this:

"Ma'am, whatever I tell you today, I'm going to do it, and I will not stop until you've got all your money."

There was this long pause. Then she whispered, "Wow."

I could tell by that one word that she was not used to people with integrity.

Proverbs 22:1 says, *"A good name is rather to be chosen than great riches."* Your word should be your bond. Make every effort to uphold the agreement you make with your creditors. They keep notes of every phone call you make to them. If you need to change the payment arrangement you agreed upon, call them again and explain your situation. But say it in a positive voice. Proverbs 15:1 says, *"A soft answer turneth away wrath."* They are much more willing to work with you if you're proactive and pleasant than if their records show that you called sixty-two times and lied about what you were going to do.

PAYING DOWN DEBT

Your next goal should be paying down your debt. At this stage of the game, paying it down feels a little less daunting than paying it off. You can start by doing things to free up more money. Liquidate a few items. Sell a car. Sell some jewelry. You know you don't even need all that stuff. Have a garage sale. I googled and found out that the average person makes $650 in a garage sale. That could be a good start toward paying down your debt.

You'd be amazed at how many ways you can free up money. Linda and I had two landlines in our house for twenty years. It hit us one day that we both had cell phones and hadn't used those landlines in fifteen years. So why pay AT&T? Canceling the landlines allowed us to sow even more money into the new church we wanted to build.

On top of the phone bill, we saved another $60 a month by buying a package of Dunkin' Donuts coffee to brew at home instead of going through the drive-through every day. I'm a

Dunkin' coffee freak. If I can do this, then surely you can make some small sacrifice to live below your budget and free up more money to pay down debt.

Some people use the equity on their home to pay down debt. Home equity lines of credit are better than revolving charge cards. But if you're going to take out a home equity line of credit, you're really going to need some discipline and restraint. Linda and I took out a $75,000 home equity line of credit, and we paid off all our credit cards, which was wonderful. We celebrated. It was great. I remember starting to pay off that line of credit. I'd pay off $400, then go get $200 of it back. Over time, I paid it off, but I went back to the bank and said, "I need $23,000 back." They gave it to me. I started paying it off, and the same thing happened again. After that, I told the bank, "Block me. Don't let me take one more dollar out of here. If I come in, say no. Don't answer me. Don't talk to me. Don't let me transfer money from one account to the other because I'm hurting myself."

I'm trying to teach you how to get to the place where when the Holy Spirit says, "Give a hundred dollars to the ministry," you have space to breathe.

Before you graduate from paying *down* debt to paying *off* debt, you will have to get rid of that grasshopper mentality. That's the mind-set that says, "I'm so small and my bills are so high. I owe Visa and Citibank so much. It's just little old me trying to pay all of this." If God is on your side, you're going to make it, because He's more than the world against you.

Before you graduate from paying down debt to paying off debt, you will have to get rid of that grasshopper mentality. That's the mind-set that says, "I'm so small and my bills are so high. I owe Visa and Citibank so much. It's just little old me trying to pay all of this." If God is on your side, you're going to make it!

The first key to the payoffs is to pay the minimum amount due every month, on every card, on time. When you aren't used to paying at all, paying on time is a struggle. We were so far behind that we weren't paying anything on our credit cards. But you have to pay, and you have to do it on time. This prevents creditors from loading your account with penalties and fees that inflate the amount you owe.

Let's say that you maxed out a $5,000 credit card and you didn't pay it on time last month. Your minimum payment is $250 a month. They're going to hit you with an additional $39 fee because you paid late. Then they're going to pop you with another $39 penalty if you're over your card's limit. So you've racked up an extra $78 on your payment just because you missed the last payment by one day. And we can't forget the interest. Lawmakers capped it so that credit card companies cannot charge more than 49.9 percent interest, but that's an astronomical amount.

In this example, you have to pay $328 ($250 of your payment and $78 in miscellaneous charges). Do that every month, and you'll shell out over $900 in fees in a year, and not one penny of that will go toward the principal. Jesus, help us!

When Linda and I had twenty-three maxed-out credit cards, something in the parable of the talents convicted me about debt.

> *For unto every one that hath shall be given, and he shall have abundance: but from him that hath not shall be taken away even that which he hath.*   (Matthew 25:29)

Have you ever seen somebody who just keeps receiving favor after favor? That's because God watches how people handle finances, and He releases more if they are good stewards.

> *God watches how people handle finances, and He releases more if they are good stewards.*

I realized that we had to get out from under the load of debt so we could honor God in our finances. Linda and I stopped using all of our credit cards, even the ones we didn't cut up. Every time we would begin to pay a card off, I would dedicate it to God and say, "God, when this is paid off, You're going to get the glory. You're going to get the honor." Then I would put it in a place of prayer, generally in my Bible.

ENTER THE MATRIX

Then God gave me a matrix of how I was to get out of debt. This matrix only shows fourteen months of progress, but if you follow it, you can pay off $2,000 in four months, $6,000 in fourteen months, and you will be completely debt-free from $25,000 in credit card debt in sixty months. This is the final way I paid off credit cards after I failed to get debt-free with a home equity loan I had taken out earlier.

I have included this matrix beginning on page 91, but I want to explain it to you simply. Suppose you have five credit cards. Let's say each one of them has a $5,000 balance, and you have $500 per month to pay on all of them. The minimum monthly payment on each of them is $35. Of course, you're going to follow the number one rule, which is to pay the minimum due on each one of those cards every month on time. That comes out to $175. What do you do with the remaining $325 you set aside for credit card payments?

Most of us would be tempted to spread it out evenly between the five cards. But if you give each card $100 ($35 minimum due plus $65 extra) a month, you've done nothing. The fastest way to make a dent in your debt is to apply that extra $325 to one card. Check your statements to see which card has the highest interest. That's where you want to put that extra $325. Between the minimum payment and the extra payment, you'll be paying a total of $360 each month on that card. In fifteen months, your high-interest card will be completely paid off. All the while, you will have avoided late fees and over-the-limit fees on the other four cards.

Now you start on the credit card with the second highest interest and repeat the process until you've paid them all. It averages out to you being completely debt-free in sixty months—five years. But the key is that you have to start with the credit card that has the highest interest. That's key. And I can't stress enough that, of course, you can't use the cards.

Some people feel they need to pay off the smallest balance first to stay motivated. But that doesn't work in your favor to the same degree. Suppose your Visa has a $3,000 balance with 22 percent interest, and your Mastercard has a $1,500 balance with 12 percent interest. Which one will be easier and quicker to pay off? Most would be tempted to pay the Mastercard first because the balance and interest are smaller. But remember, the key is the interest. If you discipline yourself to pay off the higher interest card first, in thirty-nine months, both cards will have zero balances, and you will have paid $1,283 in interest between the two cards. If you pay off the lower interest card first, it will take you forty-two months to pay both cards off, and you will pay a total of $1,764 in interest. By disciplining yourself to pay off the higher interest card first, you'll save $481 in interest and pay the cards off three months sooner than if you paid off the smaller interest card first.

You decide—do you really need the motivation that comes from seeing small debts go first, even if it's at the expense of spending more money on interest and taking longer to pay it off?

God kept bringing me back to the importance of sowing into the kingdom during this entire process. You have to plant for a harvest to come in. God will not violate His Word; He honors it.

Here's the testimony of a couple who reaped the benefits of faithful sowing. I'd been these folks' pastor for thirty years when they shared this. They'd done a budget before I taught on faith and finances, but all it told them was that they didn't bring in enough money to pay their bills. However, they always paid their tithes and offering. And guess what? Their bills were always paid on time. They'd never gone hungry. Only God can make dollars stretch like that, and all because they were faithful stewards and givers no matter what.

> *Bring ye all the tithes into the storehouse, that there may be meat in mine house, and prove me now herewith, saith the LORD of hosts, if I will not open you the windows of heaven, and pour you out a blessing, that there shall not be room enough to receive it. And I will rebuke the devourer for your sakes.* (Malachi 3:10–11)

God says to bring the tenth into the storehouse, and He will magnify and exponentially increase it. An assistant pastor taught that after God blows up the 10 percent, He walks over to the other 90 percent and protects it from the devourer. Some of you are working three jobs and still can't survive. It's because God has not put a hedge of protection around your finances. He said, "If you bring Me what's Mine, I'll protect what's yours."

> *Some of you are working three jobs and still can't survive. It's because God has not put a hedge of protection around your finances. He said, "If you bring Me what's Mine, I'll protect what's yours."*

I am walking in more favor right now than I've ever had in my life. Blessings have chased me down and overtaken me. (See Deuteronomy 28:2.) I once told my son-in-law when he picked me up from the airport, "I'm walking in so much favor that I feel dangerous." While walking through the airport to catch my flight home, a manager in one of the coffeehouses had handed me a Frappuccino and said, "Sir, we're teaching these kids how to make these drinks. Here. It's on the house." That's favor.

A notable Christian network called and said, "Pastor Dan, we've heard of you, and we want you to appear on our international broadcast show." That's the favor of God at work. After my first appearance, they invited me back again and again. Favor. I've been blessed to travel to the nations and minister side by side with Pastor Benny Hinn in his healing crusades. Favor.

It all comes down to a desire to honor God through stewardship. My dear friend Richard Roberts once told the story about a family who found some hundred-year-old seeds while cleaning out an old barn that their grandparents had owned. They took the seeds and said, "Wonder what would happen if we plant them?" They planted them in the soil. Guess what happened? The seeds sprung up and produced a harvest. Why? Because a seed is still a seed, no matter how long it's been sitting around. If you plant a seed, a harvest will come.

PRAYER

Heavenly Father, give me the strength to face my financial condition with boldness. Take away fear, shame, anxiety, and depression. With You, all things are possible! Thank You for helping me to learn better and to do better. Thank You for helping me to make wise choices that honor You. I want to be debt-free. I want to be a blessing to others around me, so I thank You for the strength and resources to do so. In Jesus's name, amen.

4

STEP 4:
HOW TO SAVE

We're going to talk about getting into the habit of saving. When you learn to save money, you reverse the curse on your life, and you get in the right position to receive favor.

The Bible says you are the lender, not the borrower. (See Deuteronomy 28:12.) When you're in the position of borrowing, you're subordinate to everybody. Think about it. Anytime you owe somebody money, you have to be nice to that person, even if he or she makes it hard to do so. Haven't you had enough stress in your life because of finances? Reverse the curse and get yourself in the position that the Scripture says you should be in. Save something up so that you can lend to somebody instead of borrowing.

I don't care if you've only got four hundred dollars in the savings account. Perhaps you feel good about it and tell everybody about your little four hundred dollars. It's not four hundred thousand dollars, but you've got something put away, and suddenly the stress begins to lift off you.

A SPIRITUAL PRINCIPLE

Saving is a spiritual principle in the Bible.

On the first day of every week, each one of you should set aside a sum of money in keeping with your income, saving it up, so that when I come no collections will have to be made.
(1 Corinthians 16:2 NIV)

Go to the ant, thou sluggard; consider her ways, and be wise: which having no guide, overseer or ruler, provideth her meat in the summer and gathereth her food in the harvest.
(Proverbs 6:6–8)

The ant has nobody telling her what to do, but look at what she does—she saves. She stores up. That's what a wise man does.

Wise people store up the best food and olive oil. But foolish people eat up everything they have. (Proverbs 21:20 NIRV)

A wise man learns how to put something in reserve, but a foolish man spends everything he's got. Give a kid five dollars, and he is headed to the candy store or somewhere to buy something he wants. The last thing he thinks about is how long he can save it. His mother might say what some of our mothers said to us: "Do you have to spend every dollar you get? Is it burning a hole in your pocket?"

Genesis 41 tells the story of Joseph interpreting Pharaoh's dream and being brought to the storeroom to save during seven years of plenty so that when seven years of famine came, there would be enough provision to not only feed the Egyptians but also to sell to other nations.

In addition, Jesus taught dozens of parables in the Word of God, and half of them dealt with money. In the parable of the talents in Matthew 25, the man who was given five talents invested them and was able to give his master ten talents when he returned. The one who had been given two talents likewise doubled the money. But the man who had been given one talent buried it. When the lord of the house came back, two of the men handed him back the talents he had given them, with interest. The master said to them, *"Well done, good and faithful servant"* (Matthew 25:23) and rewarded them, making them rulers *"over many things."*

WHEN FAVOR COMES TO YOU

When you get yourself in the proper position, you no longer have to chase favor; favor comes to you. Some of us chase down jobs, titles, positions, and relationships. But I've learned that when I line up with the Word of God, get under the covering of the ministry, and get in covenant with God's people, the right blessings come into my life.

I've learned that when I line up with the Word of God, get under the covering of the ministry, and get in covenant with God's people, the right blessings come into my life.

I can't even begin to tell you all the favor going on in my life. In one year, I taped hundreds of episodes of a television show. I loved it, but I was experiencing favor overload. I would barely make it through the doors and they'd be offering me some new opportunity. I finally had to say, "No, no more. I can't handle any more favor."

When I went to check into my hotel during one of my trips to shoot that television show, the lady at the front desk said, "Pastor Dan, you're in Room 900."

As I got on the elevator, I thought, *I'll bet that's a room right by the elevator, where I'll hear people running up and down the hall all night.* When the elevator opened, I saw a set of double doors with a sign that said presidential suite. I stepped inside and couldn't believe my eyes. I'd never stayed in anything of that caliber. I called the front desk and said, "You gave me the wrong room."

She said, "No, someone booked that room for you and paid it in full."

Favor! This was forty years in the making. All that time, I kept going to church and doing what I do—preaching, singing, and praising God—even when hardly anybody was there. I got in the right position, and favor came. Get yourself in the right position!

You may feel like you have messed up your life so badly that somebody ought to slap you. But when you get yourself lined up with God, it doesn't take as long for Him to fix you as it did for you to mess yourself up. He restores the years the locust and the cankerworm have eaten. (See Joel 1:4.) Get yourself in order. Get yourself lined up with God, and a year from now, you won't even recognize where you are.

BENEFITS OF SAVING

Let's talk more about saving. I have heard that 88 percent of Americans have no savings. Half of American families are living paycheck to paycheck, and many have borrowed so much money that they can't see a way out. Do you know that if you borrow $10,000 at 9 percent interest for ten years, you're going to pay back $15,884? But if you were to save $10,000 for that same amount of time, it would grow to almost $24,000. Catch the revelation?

Saving Builds Security

There are so many advantages to saving. It provides security for rainy-day situations. Having money saved up also allows you to do what you want to do, when you want to do it. Wouldn't you like to be able to do something this week that you've really been wanting to do, and not have to juggle or skip bills to do it? Saving can lead to a whole different lifestyle because you reverse the curse.

Saving Builds Character

Saving money also builds character. A person disciplined enough to save money can grow and mature. It gives you power over your life. Opportunities are available. Giving becomes effortless. You're able to sow seed in the ministry.

Let me really blow your mind with a little compound interest calculation. Compound interest is much better than simple interest. Simple interest is calculated based on the amount of your original investment. Compound interest is calculated based on the amount of your original investment plus the interest you've already accrued. Now let's look at a scenario. Let's say you start with $500 as an investment and you add only $500 ($10 a week) to it every year. If you let your investment grow for twenty years in a mutual fund at 6 percent interest compounded annually, it will increase to $21,000. That's just from saving $40 dollars a month, or $10 dollars a week, for twenty years.[2]

Young people have more time to do this than some of us. Don't you wish you had started this earlier? If a young person puts $500 in a mutual fund at 6 percent interest compounded annually, and only adds $500 ($10 a week) to it each year, they will have $120,000 forty-five years later.

What if you upped the ante and started with $500 in savings, then added $50 a week instead of $10? You could set up an automatic deduction to come out of your check weekly. Do this for twenty years, and you will have $103,000. Do it for forty-five years, and you'll end up with over $593,000. This isn't hocus-pocus. You can Google search an online compound interest calculator to plug your own numbers into.

You might be saying, "This is all fine and good, Pastor Dan, but I don't have any extra money to invest in savings." Most of us have it; we just don't know where to look for it.

I'm a hot dog lover. (Here I go again, confessing all my sins!) Last week, I bought two hot dogs with chili cheese, hot peppers, and seasoning salt, costing $6.67. Then I picked up my Dunkin' Donuts coffee for $2.90. In that thirty-minute trip, I spent $10.

---

2. To calculate your own compound interest savings goals, the government provides this online calculator: https://www.investor.gov/additional-resources/free-financial-planning-tools/compound-interest-calculator.

If I went without the hot dogs and coffee just one day a week, I could fulfill Scripture by saving $10 every week for a year. By the end of five years, if I didn't add anything else to it, it would come out to over $3,600 with interest. After forty years of sacrificing hot dogs and coffee just once each week, I'd have $121,000. That's enough to live in retirement for two years without a penny from Social Security or any other source. Plus, I'd be healthier from eating fewer hot dogs and drinking less coffee!

Ten dollars a week can help secure your future and put you in a whole different place in just a few years. But it comes down to this spiritual principle:

> *He that hath no rule over his own spirit is like a city that is broken down, and without walls.*   (Proverbs 25:28)

One translation says a person who can't rule over his own spirit is like a city that doesn't have a police force. You've got to come to a point where you don't need the pastor or anybody else to check you because you check yourself. That puts you back in the right position. Discipline yourself to save at least $10 a week. Start there if that's where you have to start. But start somewhere.

FOUR PRINCIPLES FOR BEING DEBT FREE

Let's review the first four principles of becoming debt-free.

Number One: Stop Spending

Shred the credit cards. If you are going to be successful in life, if you are going to be who God says you are (the lender and not the borrower), opt out of spending.

Number Two: Get on a Budget

I don't care what it takes; you have to get on a budget.

Number Three: Follow the Payoff Plan

Put all your credit cards into the matrix I created and follow it. You'll be able to see exactly how long it will take you to pay everything off.

Number Four: Save

You have to learn how to save. Think about what your testimony would be if you could be the lender and not the borrower. People in our congregation have sown and sown into ministry, and their testimony is so powerful because they've learned how to give and to position themselves with a budget so that they save enough to live in prosperity.

SOWING FOR INCREASE

One powerful principle I've mentioned in every step is to sow seed for increase. God honors you when you do what His Word says and bring the firstfruits into the house of God. This is a revelation God gave me on sowing seed for increase.

> *Joshua set up twelve stones in the midst of Jordan, in the place where the feet of the priests which bare the ark of the covenant stood: and they are there unto this day.*
>
> (Joshua 4:9)

The children of Israel were getting ready to cross over the Jordan River, which had a terrible reputation. It was extremely cold, muddy, and treacherous. Everybody was afraid of the Jordan. Nobody wanted to go across it. But God told the Israelites that before they could get to the Promised Land, they would have to go through the Jordan River. There was no bridge, helicopter, or boat. The Promised Land was on the other side of the biggest trouble they'd ever faced.

God commanded the priests to go stand in the middle of the Jordan. Each of the twelve tribes of Israel was to appoint one man who was charged with the task of putting a polished rock on his shoulder. When the priests' feet hit the waters of the Jordan River, God rolled the river back, and each of the twelve men took his rock and put it in the middle of the dry Jordan riverbed. Because they didn't have paper currency like us, the polished rocks served as their seed offering.

Until God rolled the waters back, the Jordan River had only stood for trouble. But when they planted that offering in the midst of a place called trouble, they walked into the Promised Land.

There comes a moment in life (and I know this as well as I know my name) when you have to say, "I'm in the midst of trouble. I'm in the middle of a treacherous, cold, and muddy Jordan. But today I'm walking in the Jordan, and I'm laying down an offering in the middle of trouble." When you do that, the Jordan is rolled back in your life, and never again will it stand for trouble.

PRAYER

Lord, we thank you for revelation on saving. We purpose in our hearts to discipline ourselves to save, so that we can bless the kingdom. Father, we desire to be rich not only financially but spiritually. Jesus, come into our hearts and cleanse us of all our sins. We give Your name the glory. In Jesus's name, amen.

5

STEP 5:
REPAIRERS OF THE BREACH

When I first taught the faith and finances series to my church, I thought I was finished after four weeks. I made a plan, but God had another plan. Proverbs 16:9 says that a man plans his course in his heart but that the Lord determines his steps.

God had me teach on faith and finances again three years later. By that time, I was personally charged about giving. It's like everything God put in my hand—I just wanted to give it right back. I had been in ministry for thirty-two years at that point, and I'd never been in such a giving mode.

Miracles started happening in our congregation. Praise reports were coming in left and right. One letter said this:

> Pastor Dan, thank you for listening when God said to teach this series. I kept my promise to God to plant a one-hundred-dollar seed, and God has done

supernatural blessings for me already. I invited a bunch of people who had no job to come to church with me. The next week, everybody who came to church with me had a job!

It wasn't just financial blessings that were coming. One Sunday, fifty-five people waited in line after service for prayer. On another Sunday, I received an email saying,

> Nobody knew this, but for the past three months, I've been going to the doctor for one test after another. I finally had surgery two weeks ago. They took a biopsy because they thought it was cancer of the cervix. I received the report last Friday, and it said the test came back clear. No cancer! The blood of Jesus covered me. As you know, I work at Cardinal Bernadine Cancer Center at Loyola. I don't even care to tell you about the sadness I see every day at work. But I'm thankful. Once again, God has covered me! So I'm ready to get back to work for Jesus.

If you seek God first and His righteousness, you won't have to chase your dreams; your dreams will chase you. I believe that happens because God is watching even when we think nobody is looking. At times, I've been in this church preaching when I thought nobody was listening and nobody cared. I was just showing up. Just being on the job and doing what I was supposed to do. I thought nobody was watching me, but God was setting me up for future blessings.

People in our congregation weren't just receiving blessings on an individual level. The ministry as a whole was being blessed beyond measure. Lighthouse made international headlines one week in 2009. I was asked to appear on CBS, Fox News, and Moody Radio. I was also in the *Chicago Tribune* and the *Chicago Sun-Times*. All this came about because Lighthouse was blessing people. We were giving folks money. And would you believe some people criticized us for doing that? Guess who the biggest critics were? Other pastors! How could they be against us blessing people?

Before going on air for an interview with Fox Network in New York, the interviewer said, "Pastor, I've got to tell you, we've had a hard time figuring out how to do this show with you this morning because when we have pastors on the news, it's usually because they have gotten in trouble for stealing money from the church. But you're giving thousands and thousands of dollars away. We all are trying to figure out how to spin this story."

REPAIR AND RESTORE

God wants you to experience that kind of increase, so I'm going to talk about restoration and being repairers of the breach.

Then shalt thou call, and the Lord shall answer; thou shalt cry, and he shall say, Here I am. If thou take away from the midst of thee the yoke, the putting forth of the finger, and speaking vanity; and if thou draw out thy soul to the hungry, and satisfy the afflicted soul; then shall thy light rise in obscurity, and thy darkness be as the noon day: and the Lord shall guide thee continually, and satisfy thy soul in drought, and make fat thy bones: and thou shalt be like a watered garden, and like a spring of water, whose waters fail not. And they that shall be of thee shall build the old waste places: thou shalt raise up the foundations of many generations; and thou shalt be called, The repairer of the breach, The restorer of paths to dwell in.   (Isaiah 58:9–12)

When the Bible talks about us being repairers of the breach, it's talking about restoration. Unless you understand restoration and how God feels about it, you can't restore your finances. What did Jesus come to this earth to do? He became a living sacrifice so that you and I could be restored back to God. The number one reason Jesus came was not for you to have a better car or a bigger house. The first reason He came was to restore what had been broken in the garden of Eden and put you back together with God. God's agenda is restoration for your life.

The number one reason Jesus came was not for you to have a better car or a bigger house. The first reason He came was to restore what had been broken in the garden of Eden and put you back together with God. God's agenda is restoration for your life.

Go to the Word. Blinded eyes restored. Lame legs restored. God has a way of taking things that were broken and putting them back together. Am I talking to anybody who understands? Some of you have lost careers, respect, jobs, your love life, and finances. I prophesy that God is about to restore it, with interest.

God can physically restore you. God can relationally restore you. God can positionally restore you. God can financially restore you.

> *I will restore to you the years that the locust hath eaten, the cankerworm, and the caterpiller, and the palmerworm, my great army which I sent among you. And ye shall eat in plenty, and be satisfied, and praise the name of the LORD your God, that hath dealt wondrously with you: and my people shall never be ashamed.* (Joel 2:25–26)

Some of you need to restore your relationship with your mother or father. For fifteen years, I didn't speak to my father. Finally, God said to me, "Your daddy is not your issue. You didn't make him. You don't have a heaven or hell to send him to. You are troubled, Dan Willis, because you stand up and preach, yet you don't speak to your own father. I am always about restoration. You can't preach something you don't live by."

I remember the day that I picked up the phone and called my father. I said, "Dad, you've done nothing to me. I have not spoken to you, and I'm going to ask you to forgive me."

Very soon after that, things that I could not have imagined began to happen in my life. A large book publisher in America called me and asked, "Why don't you write a book?"

Then they said, "Why don't you write three more books? And while you're at it, why don't you write one on faith and finances since you're an expert on that?"

Really? I was broke.

I trace all that back to the day I restored my relationship with my father. Recording contracts, book contracts, and television programs all were opened up to me the day I restored things with my father.

Linda and I will celebrate forty years of marriage this year. Do you know how many times we have had to bring restoration to our marriage in that time? Don't get me started. Pastors aren't immune to challenges in their marriages. Where there are people, there are issues. We had to make up our minds many years ago that it's okay if there are some things we don't agree on. We can't expect the other to do and say everything our way. We had to learn to love our similarities and respect our differences to bring restoration to the situation. The very purpose of Jesus was to restore.

> *The thief cometh not, but for to steal, and to kill, and to destroy: I am come that they might have life, and that they might have it more abundantly.*   (John 10:10)

HAVING THE INTEGRITY TO MAKE RESTITUTION

Financial restoration begins with a conviction in your heart that being in debt offends heavenly principles and your integrity. From there, you must begin making restitution to those to whom you owe money. Even if you are bankrupt and owe your mama, auntie, best friend, boo, and everybody else, get right with people, and you'll be right with God.

Some of you may have filed for bankruptcy and now live with that hanging over you. I'm not here to do bankruptcy, "beat you up" church. I'm here to teach you this principle: bankruptcy should never be your first option. It used to be that you couldn't get a credit card for a while after you went bankrupt. Now, you can get credit cards three weeks after you file. Some people get out of one frying pan and into the next. Please let me help you. Restoration is the spiritual issue. God said you'll live in plenty and you'll never be ashamed. But it starts with restoration.

> *Therefore if thou bring thy gift to the altar, and there remem-berest that thy brother hath ought against thee; leave there thy gift before the altar, and go thy way; first be reconciled to thy brother, and then come and offer thy gift.*
> (Matthew 5:23–24)

God said that if you bring your gift to the altar and remember that there are problems between you and somebody else, you are to leave your gift at the altar and go make peace with that person. I started wondering why God said to leave your gift at the altar while you go make peace. Why didn't He say to go make peace and then come back with your offering? At first, I thought that He knew a lot of folks who would not make it back to the altar after dealing with some of the hard-hearted people they had issues with, so He was getting their offering before they left. But I don't believe that's why God did it.

Restoration is the spiritual issue. God said you'll live in plenty and you'll never be ashamed. But it starts with restoration.

In the book of Genesis, when Jacob came to Esau, he took a bunch of gifts. (See Genesis 32–33.) He and his brother had

had a rift and were estranged from each other. Prior to meeting his brother, Jacob sent all kinds of flocks and cattle to make restitution. Before he arrived to offer his brother the right hand of fellowship, he sent a gift. Why did Jacob send a gift? For the same reason that Jesus said to leave your gift at the altar and seek peace before returning to the altar. He knew that true worship is enhanced when relationships are put back together. If you want to hear Jesus more clearly and you want God to really start blessing you in your life, work out your differences with the person whom you haven't spoken to in a while.

It's not just about repairing your credit. It's about repairing your spiritual condition. To not repair and restore things in your life is a spiritual condition. How can you say you love God, whom you have not seen, and you can't stand your brother whom you have seen?

The Bible talks about restoration eight hundred times. Jesus came to restore everything in your life that the devil has taken. But God is not just about restoration—He's about restoration with increase.

> *Men do not despise a thief, if he steal to satisfy his soul when he is hungry; but if he be found, he shall restore sevenfold; he shall give all the substance of his house.*
>
> (Proverbs 6:30–31)

God never restores just what you had. He restores with interest everything the devil stole from you. If you seek first the kingdom of God and His righteousness (see Matthew 6:33), God will make the thief go bring it back with sevenfold increase.

Nobody has anything in God for which he or she has not had to fight, throw some devils out, and prophesy to himself or herself. It's work to get things right, but you've got to repair. You've got to restore. Statistics say that 42 percent of marital issues come from finances. Sixty percent of divorces are because of financial issues. Seventy percent of Americans run out of money before the end of the month, usually by the second or third week of the month. And we're escalating in debt. Eighty-eight percent of Americans have no savings. Within ten years of retirement, 50 percent of Americans have less than two thousand dollars saved. We are so messed up in this, and the only thing that can straighten us out is God's Word. His Word is a lamp to our feet and a light to our path. (See Psalm 119:105.) It will illuminate the way so we can walk out of this situation.

STEPS TO RESTORING YOUR CREDIT

Now let's talk about credit repair. Here are some steps to take to get good credit.

1. Review your credit report. You can pull a free credit report (minus your credit score) once a year from www.freecreditreport.com. It's important for you to know your credit score because that's what lenders use to determine how much of a risk it would be to loan money to you. This website will charge you five dollars for your credit score, but it's a worthwhile investment. An average score is 723. You want to be above that. Ladies, if a guy wants to date you, make sure he has

a good credit score! If you worked to get your credit score to 735 and his is 241, that's a red flag!

Here are some common questions people have been asking me about credit reports. How long does bad stuff stay on my credit? Seven years. How long does bankruptcy stay on my credit? Ten years, and even then, you may have to request that they take it off.

2.   Next, get a binder. I'm very organized. In that binder, I documented every phone call I made to creditors and every letter I wrote to them. When I got on the phone with them, if they gave me some wrong information, I would say, "Oh, no, on January 8, I wrote this letter, and on August 8, I spoke to Cecilia."

Half the time, they would just say, "Okay, what do you want?" because I'd been keeping better notes than they had. Keep a dispute binder.

3.   Send your disputes online. Don't do it old-school. Don't mail a letter to the credit reporting agencies. It's ineffective. They do everything online, so send your dispute in online. The goal is to create positive information on your report. Many people want to delete stuff. Repairing it is what raises your credit score because you have to have information on there to establish yourself, so creditors can see that even though you messed up, you made a comeback. The goal should not be to delete but to repair.

4. Wait for the response, which can take two to three months.

5. When it comes back, carefully read everything on it, including any symbols that might be on it.

6. Know when you're most likely to get a positive response from creditors. November and December are the best times. Lenders are more apt to be forgiving and work with you during the holiday season. That's a good time to ask them to fix something on your credit.

7. Don't be afraid to dispute it again.

8. Write another letter to the creditor if you have to. You can write this one longhand if you would prefer, after you have submitted the initial request online.

9. Don't threaten to sue a credit reporting agency. Threatening them is a federal offense. Lying to them is a federal crime for which you can serve time. Make sure everything you tell them is the truth because they will check it out. If you threaten to sue them, make sure to first call an attorney to find out if you have a case. One way to do that is to belong to a prepaid legal program. I've belonged to one for almost thirty years. Although creditors want to avoid being sued because they have to spend so much money in litigation, if you do decide to sue them, they will put your feet to the fire. So really count the cost when making your decision.

PRAYER

Dear Lord Jesus, I now know I must be restored to my fellow man. I come to You for forgiveness. I repent. Please forgive me for every sin in my life. I renounce it. I reject it. I do not want it. I only want You, Jesus. Please come into my heart. Restore everything that's been taken from me, Lord. Restore love. Restore joy. Restore peace. Restore my family, relationships, and finances. But most of all, restore me to You, dear Lord. In Jesus's name, amen.

6

USING GIFTS AND WISDOM TO GAIN WEALTH

I came to wrestle the enemy out of your life and to let you know that God has plans for your life. If you have an entrepreneurial spirit and want to be a business owner, I'm coming down your alley with a checklist for starting your own business.

You might have been thinking about it for a long time, but God had a divine order to your life. Proverbs 16:9 says, *"A man's heart deviseth his way: but the LORD directeth his steps."* When you do things out of order, they get messed up.

For example, a woman in our church said, "Pastor Dan, I've got to tell you how God spared my life. The horn on my car has been broken for a while, and I kept saying I had to get it repaired. But I kept putting it off because every time I saved enough money for it, another more important car part broke that I had to get fixed."

Personally, I don't know how she functioned without a horn on her car. Some of us use our horn more than we use our brakes. You know who you are. You're the ones at the red light blowing at the car in front of you as soon as the light turns green.

Anyway, she told me, "I woke up one morning, and God said, 'Today is the day. Get that horn in order.' It was the strangest thing. I drove to my mechanic, and he fixed the horn. A couple hours after he'd fixed it, I was sitting at a red light, blocked in traffic in the middle lane, when an eighteen-wheeler in front of me all of a sudden shifted into reverse and started coming at my little car. I hit that horn, and had it been two hours earlier, it would not have made a sound. But because I'd listened to that still, small voice telling me to get it in order, that eighteen-wheeler didn't hit me. God's timing was perfect, and He spared my life."

Today I'm about to blow the horn because there's an 18-wheeler threatening to back up on somebody. Today is your day to stop talking about putting a business in place. You're not getting any younger. I came to empower you so you can learn to use your gifts and your wisdom to gain wealth.

Wealth means the state of being rich and affluent; having a plentiful supply of material goods and money. The Bible says that God is the source of wealth.

> *Thou shalt remember the* LORD *thy God: for it is he that giveth thee power to get wealth, that he may establish his covenant.*   (Deuteronomy 8:18)

The covenant referred to here is God's promise that His people would be the head and not the tail, the lender and not the borrower. It's plain as pie. God says, "In order to keep my covenant with you, I'm going to give you wisdom to gain wealth." Wisdom is accumulated knowledge or experience, with common sense and insight. True wisdom is a combination of studying to show yourself approved and seasoning it with some common sense. Solomon said, *"I applied mine heart to know, and to search, and to seek out wisdom"* (Ecclesiastes 7:25). We should do the same. After all, what's the sense in God giving you wealth if you don't know how to make it last? We read about people winning the lottery, then not knowing how to keep the money.

> *What's the sense in God giving you wealth if you don't know how to make it last?*

Some of us work two or three jobs chasing after wealth and still have nothing. In Luke 5, Simon and the other fishermen were toiling, doing what they could do, but nothing worked until they listened to what God said to do.

> *Simon answering said unto him, Master, we have toiled all the night, and have taken nothing: nevertheless at thy word I will let down the net.* (Luke 5:5)

You might be burning the candle at both ends, but if you would just stop, make God your source, and listen to His wisdom, you'll be able to succeed at your gifting and release the kingdom wealth that He's placed inside of you.

You say, "Well, Pastor Dan, how can that be? I don't have any gifts or talents." I'm going to believe the Word over what you think. The Bible says God is no respecter of persons. (See Acts 10:34.) That means you have a seed for some talent in you.

RECOGNIZING YOUR TALENTS

You may recall that in the parable of the talents, the wise master gave five talents to one steward, two to another, and one to another. In those days, the definition of talent was twofold.

First, it meant a natural ability inside of you that allowed you to obtain wealth. God gave to each person a natural ability to resource something inside of him or her to gain wealth. Some talents are hidden; others are more expressive. But everybody has at least one.

I was raised by an old-school mother who used to tell me, "Son, God gave you a talent. If you don't use that talent for God, He'll take it from you and give it to somebody else." I used to think that was just my mother speaking, until I had an aha moment. I realized that what she was saying came straight out of Matthew 25. The guy who had been given five talents doubled it. The guy who had been given a couple of talents doubled his. But what did the steward with one talent do? He buried it in the earth. When the master came back, he said, "You buried your talent. You hid your natural resource to obtain wealth in the earth. I will take back the talent I gave to you and give it to him who has proven himself capable of handling talent."

Now, the second definition of a talent blew my mind. When Jesus walked the earth, a talent was equivalent to fifteen years of wages. So the steward who had been given five talents actually received seventy-five years of wages at one time. The second steward received two talents, or thirty years of wages, all at once. That's a big deal!

The last was given one talent, or fifteen years of wages. So if you make $30,000 a year, that would be like someone walking up to you, handing you $450,000, and saying, "Here, do a little something with this." How many could handle that? The man in the parable couldn't. He took $450,000 and buried it in the ground. The master came back and said, "Because you did nothing with the talent I gave you, I'm going to extract it from you and give it to the guy who has seventy-five years' worth of wages."

You better use your talent for the Lord. All throughout Scripture, people used talents to gain resources and wealth. Peter used his talent as a fisherman. Dorcas from Joppa was a seamstress. The woman in Proverbs 31 used her skills to bless her family. Joseph was a carpenter. The principle is this: God put a talent in you, and your increase will always be tied to that talent.

Too many of us are sitting around waiting for somebody to walk up and write us a check. Most of the time, you're going to have to look for the talent within you to not only become debt-free but to access the kingdom wealth that God has got with your name on it.

Too many of us are sitting around waiting for somebody to walk up, write us a check, and say, "Here, pay off your mortgage. Pay off your car loan. Pay off your Visa. Pay off your Mastercard.

Pay off your Macy's card. Pay off your Target card." Good for you if someone pays it off for you! But most of the time, you're going to have to look for the talent within you to not only become debt-free but to access the kingdom wealth that God has got with your name on it.

You could be jealous of someone else's talent, but why? Your talent is not theirs, and theirs is not yours. But inside of you is the key to kingdom wealth.

You might be saying, "Pastor Dan, I don't know what mine is." You have to look! You better stir the pot until it comes to the surface. Everybody has been given a talent somewhere along the line. I started thinking about people in the church who found their talent and are using it to create wealth so they do not have to be indebted to anyone:

+ One woman learned how to quilt. I guarantee you that when she started quilting, she had a few flaws in the finished product, but she just kept doing it until she perfected it.

+ Another woman is a custom jewelry designer. I accessed her biography, and it said, "I believe that my talent is a God-given tool to help me resource wealth for the kingdom." I said, "Sister Edie, quit preaching my sermon!"

+ One man's gifting is to paint. I have to put down drop cloths, plastic, and tape for days when I paint. It looks like you're walking into a crime scene when I'm painting. But I've walked in when he was painting, and he didn't need any tape, plastic, or drop cloths because he has a steady hand and knows exactly what he's doing. He started a painting business, making tons of money.

+ I know a woman who is a lyricist, a songwriter. She started asking people if they would listen to her music. Then one of the largest churches in the world, West Angeles Church of God in Christ, in Los Angeles, California, recorded some of her songs.

+ A mother baked butter cookies and German chocolate cake. She said, "I had a man who left me with a pile of kids. I'm a single mom of four kids. I'm not going to sit around and wait on him to send me that child support check. It hasn't come yet. But what I'll do is learn how to be a Lydia. I'll learn how to be a Dorcas. I'll learn how to use the resources God put in me."

+ We have an amazing children's pastor. We can't pay her what she's worth. She has a creative gene out of this world. She paints. She does hand artwork. I couldn't do it if my life depended on it, but it comes so naturally to her because it's her gift.

See how everybody has a seed in them? Don't hate. You ought to celebrate them. God put a talent in you to help you create kingdom wealth. If you bury it, God will take it from you. When folks get mad at me because I am being blessed, I tell them, "This is not something I deserved. I get a lot of blessings by default. I was just using what I already had when God said, 'I just took this from somebody else because he wasn't using it. I'm going to place it in your hand.'"

God put a talent in you to help you create kingdom wealth. If you bury it, God will take it from you.

I want to give you some pointers as you take steps to launch your business. First, seek wisdom on using your talent.

> *God said to Solomon, Because this was in thine heart, and thou hast not asked riches, wealth, or honour, nor the life of thine enemies, neither yet hast asked long life; but hast asked wisdom and knowledge for thyself, that thou mayest judge my people, over whom I have made thee king: wisdom and knowledge is granted unto thee; and I will give thee riches, and wealth, and honour, such as none of the kings have had that have been before thee, neither shall there any after thee have the like.*   (2 Chronicles 1:11–12)

Wisdom first. Seek it out. I've always been a believer in not reinventing the wheel. Seek wisdom by watching and talking to people who have gained wealth using the same talent you're trying to develop. Want to be an author? Talk to an author. Want to be a baker? Talk to a successful baker.

Next, whatever your gift is, use it where you are. Perfect it from its infant state and use it to bless others. Practice on them. I guarantee you that anybody starting a business has given goods and services away and asked people what they thought about it. I think about our drummer. I guarantee that before he was making major money doing gigs, he was played the drums without getting paid, running around blessing people, playing for choirs, and playing for churches. You have to use it where you are.

I was raised old-school. I didn't learn how to sing at church. I learned how to sing by my mother dragging my tail from nursing home to nursing home on Saturdays. Mother would take me to three or four nursing homes, and she'd say, "Now, sing." At seven or eight years old, I'd stand up and sing.

I didn't realize that she was preparing me for years later. Lighthouse Church hasn't always been able to support me. Anybody who has started a congregation knows. The first fifteen years of my ministry, I was working two jobs and going to college. I flew all over the country singing, preaching, taking red-eye flights back, then landing at O'Hare International Airport at five in the morning to come to church and preach two or three times. Every three months, I get a royalty check because I have some CDs out and folks recorded some of my music.

Use whatever God has given you. If you sing, quit waiting for Celine Dion or Kirk Franklin to call you to do a duet. Join the choir at your church.

In addition, learn to market yourself, and do it professionally without a professional marketer. There's no excuse for your business not to succeed. Get yourself listed in some magazines. Get a website. Above all, have somebody proofread your stuff before it goes out. How is anyone supposed to think you're professional when you're handing out business cards with one phone number scratched out and another one scribbled in? You don't get a second chance to make a first impression. Market yourself professionally. The Bible says to present yourself as a living sacrifice. (See Romans 12:1.) God has always cared about presentation. If you want to succeed in business, learn to present yourself.

Sometimes you present yourself by being quiet. The Word of God says that even a fool appears to be wise when he's silent. (See Proverbs 17:28.) I was once with one of our assistant pastors when somebody asked him if his business offered various services. He was basically silent, responding with a simple, "Hmm, okay," to each of their questions—and he got the job! He told me later that as the person was asking questions, he was thinking to himself, *That's not something that I currently do, but I certainly have the ability and resources to do it, so I will.* Sometimes in marketing, less is more. Then, get a prayer agreement.

> *Again I say unto you, That if two of you shall agree on earth as touching any thing that they shall ask, it shall be done for them of my Father which is in heaven. For where two or three are gathered together in my name, there am I in the midst of them.* (Matthew 18:19–20)

I believe that businesses fail because we got the education right, we got the flyers right, we got the marketing right, but we never got a prayer intercessor on our business. You need to approach your business as if it were your ministry. Get a prayer warrior who will intercede for it. Every time I get on a plane to go preach somewhere or sing somewhere, I ask my prayer warriors to pray that when I get there, somebody will want to buy a CD or a DVD so I can make a little extra money to bring back and put into the ministry. Get some prayer agreement.

Businesses fail because we got the education right, we got the flyers right, we got the marketing right, but we never got a prayer intercessor on our business. You need to approach your business as if it were your ministry. Get a prayer warrior who will intercede for it.

Also, you have to seed for your business. The Bible says that we are to honor the Lord with our substance and with the first-fruits of all our increase. (See Proverbs 3:9.) People try to trap me by saying, "Pastor Dan, do I have to tithe on my business?"

I tell them, "You don't have to, unless you want to be obedient to God's Word and be a success." The Bible says to honor the Lord with your substance and with the firstfruits of all your increase. You want your business to be blessed? Tithe on it. God honors seed.

The Bible says that if you give sparingly, you reap sparingly, but if you give bountifully, you reap bountifully. (See 2 Corinthians 9:6.) God sees how you handle what you have. Why would He give you one hundred dollars if you don't know how to care for and be wise with ten dollars? If you run to Wal-Mart and buy shoes with every dollar you get, then you're not learning to be a wise steward with what God's giving you. But when you get a kingdom mentality and know that He's planted a seed in you to help you obtain wealth, and you're a good steward of it, God will increase you and make you the head and not the tail, the lender and not the borrower. (See Deuteronomy 28:13.)

PRAYER

Heavenly Father, thank You for breaking generational curses of poverty over my life and my family. I thank You for creative gifts, ideas, and energy to not just become debt-free but to have abundance so I can bless those around me. Thank You for this opportunity to rededicate my life and finances to You. I honor You as my Lord and Savior and give You my heart today. Thank You for salvation, grace, and freedom through Your holy Word. In Jesus's name, amen!

EPILOGUE:
RECEIVE THE INCREASE

God says you are a success. But before you are going to have financial freedom in Christ, you are going to have to see yourself as He sees you. He does not see you broken down, depressed, and impoverished. He sees you living in abundance.

> *Let them shout for joy, and be glad, that favour my righteous cause: yea, let them say continually, Let the LORD be magnified, which hath pleasure in the prosperity of his servant.*
>
> (Psalm 35:27)

Thirty years ago, I began telling people, "I'm going to be debt-free, and I'm going to give money away." Why was I saying that? Because the Bible says, *"As [a man] thinketh in his heart, so is he"* (Proverbs 23:7). I pictured this day when I was still in debt. Today I can say that Lighthouse Church has been so blessed. We're just sowing into people. My wife and I are also walking in abundance now, so much so that I go to bed every night saying, "Lord, show me who I can bless tomorrow for Your glory."

Don't think for one moment that I'm bragging about myself. If anything, I'm bragging about God. One of the greatest things that was birthed out of all those years of being so broke that I couldn't pay attention was a deep sense of gratitude for every little thing I got. I remember when we had about twenty members in a little storefront church. One of the members, Sister Racine, walked in one night with two brass offering plates she had bought at a Christian bookstore. We'd been using a hat, paper plates, and even an open Bible to take the offering. When I saw those brass offering plates, I shouted and cried. When you have nothing, you can appreciate something.

America is the most blessed country in the world, and yet we are so ungrateful for stuff. Do you want the favor of God moving in your finances? Learn to be grateful.

America is the most blessed country in the world, and yet we are so ungrateful for stuff. Do you want the favor of God moving in your finances? Learn to be grateful. Every time your boss gives you a check (I don't care if it's not what you really want it to be), take it and say, "Boss, thank you. God is good!" A grateful heart always leads to exponential increase.

Are you prepared to receive the increase? I sure wasn't at one time. If someone tried to give me something years ago, I'd say, "No, you keep it. You need it more than me."

But the Holy Spirit convicted me. He said, "I was trying to bless you, and you rejected a blessing."

I now live with an open hand and say, "All right, enlarge my territory."

Case in point, I was at a gas station one day, and a man pulled up to the fuel pump next to me. He came running over to me and asked, "Are you Pastor Dan Willis?" After he teased me a bit about the fact that he recognized me because of my hair, he asked what I was teaching at Lighthouse.

I said, "God's been talking to me about the ability to receive. He says you can't be in a position to receive until you get giving out of the way." Then I quoted Luke 6:38 to him. (*"Give and it shall be given unto you; good measure, pressed down, and shaken together, and running over, shall men give into your bosom."*)

Then I said, "God asks you to do one thing—give. But when you do that one thing, He releases six things in your favor! All of these six things happen because of your giving: *"It shall be given unto you; good measure, pressed down, and shaken together, and running over, shall men give into your bosom."*

As we stood there, I added, "The funny thing is, I woke up this morning and Holy Spirit said to believe Him for one hundred dollars today just to stretch my faith. I'm expecting somebody to give me one hundred dollars today."

The man looked at me and said, "I've got one hundred dollars in my pocket." He reached into his pocket and handed the money to me, saying, "I don't know if I'm the one or not, but here it is."

I took it and said, "You're the one, brother! You're the one!" If somebody wants to bless you, let them.

In concluding this teaching on faith and finances, I prophesy right now that you are blessed beyond measure because you are debt-free. Every credit card is paid off. Every school loan is paid off. Every car loan is paid off. Every home mortgage is paid off. As Scripture says, *"The LORD God of your fathers make you a thousand times so many more as ye are"* (Deuteronomy 1:11).

I prophesy that you will no longer bow in bondage to the earthly kingdom, where you acquiesce to words like recession and unemployment. I declare and decree that you will step into God's system, which only knows words like *"unto him that is able to keep you from falling, and to present you faultless"* (Jude 1:24) and "[the God] *that is able to do exceeding abundantly above all that we ask or think"* (Ephesians 3:20). I speak unlimited favor and increase over your life, in Jesus's name. Amen!

SAMPLE
PAYING OFF $6,000 OF DEBIT ON 3 CREDIT CARDS IN 13 MONTHS
($500/month toward payments)

	Credit Card 1	Credit Card 2	Credit Card 3
Debt	$1000	$2000	$3000
(Interest Rate divided by 12)+1	1.01	1.03	1.02
Minimum Payment	$10.00	$20.00	$20.00
Debt+Interest	$1,010.10	$2,020.60	$3,030.60
Payments	$10.00	$470.00	$20.00
Month 1	$1,000.10	$1,550.60	$3,010.60
(Interest Rate divided by 12)+1	1.01	1.03	1.02
Minimum Payment	$10.00	$20.00	$20.00
Total After Interest	$1,010.20	$1,566.57	$3,041.30
Payment	$10.00	$470.00	$20.00
Month 2	$1,000.20	$1,096.57	$3,021.30
(Interest Rate divided by 12)+1	1.01	1.03	1.02
Minimum Payment	$10.00	$20.00	$20.00
Total After Interest	$1,010.30	$1,107.86	$3,052.10
Payment	$10.00	$470.00	$20.00
Month 3	$1,000.30	$637.86	$3,032.10
(Interest Rate divided by 12)+1	1.01	1.03	1.02
Minimum Payment	$10.00	$20.00	$20.00
Total After Interest	$1,010.40	$644.42	$3,063
Payment	$10.00	$470.00	$20.00
Month 4	$1000.40	$174.42	$3,043
(Interest Rate divided by 12)+1	1.01	1.03	1.02
Minimum Payment	$10.00	$20.00	$20.00
Total After Interest	$1,010.50	$176.21	$3,074.03
Payment	$10.00	$176.21	$313.79

	Credit Card 1	Credit Card 2	Credit Card 3
Month 5	$1000.50	$0.00	$2,760.24
(Interest Rate divided by 12)+1	1.01		1.02
Minimum Payment	$10.00		$20.00
Total After Interest	$1,010.60		$2,788.39
Payment	$10.00		$490.00
Month 6	$1,000.60		$2,298.39
(Interest Rate divided by 12)+1	1.01		1.02
Minimum Payment	$10.00		$20.00
Total After Interest	$1,010.70		$2,321.83
Payment	$10.00		$490.00
Month 7	$1000.70		$1,831.51
(Interest Rate divided by 12)+1	1.01		1.02
Minimum Payment	$10.00		$20.00
Total After Interest	$1,010.80		$1,850.51
Payment	$10.00		$490.00
Month 8	$1000.80		$1,360.51
(Interest Rate divided by 12)+1	1.01		1.02
Minimum Payment	$10.00		$20.00
Total After Interest	$1,010.90		$1,374.38
Payment	$10.00		$490.00
Month 9	$1000.90		$884.38
(Interest Rate divided by 12)+1	1.01		1.02
Minimum Payment	$10.00		$20.00
Total After Interest	$1,011.00		$893.40
Payment	$10.00		$490.00

	Credit Card 1	Credit Card 2	Credit Card 3
Month 10	$1,001.00		$403.40
(Interest Rate divided by 12)+1	1.01		1.02
Minimum Payment	$10.00		$20.00
Total After Interest	$1,011.10		$411.62
Payment	$88.38		$411.62
Month 11	$922.72		$0.00
(Interest Rate divided by 12)+1	1.01		
Minimum Payment	$10.00		
Total After Interest	$932.03		
Payment	$500		
Month 12	$432.03		
(Interest Rate divided by 12)+1	1.01		
Minimum Payment	$10.00		
Total After Interest	$436.39		
Payment	$436.39		
Month 13	$0.00		

ABOUT THE AUTHOR

Dan Willis did not exactly envision a life in ministry as a young boy growing up in Chicago. Though he loved the contagious rhythms of gospel music, he never imagined that one day he'd be creating them himself. Yet from these humble beginnings developed one of today's leading pastors.

As a young boy, Dan's dreams involved entering the medical field as a neurosurgeon until the fateful day when, at age sixteen, he was called to "temporarily" take over as pastor of a local church. Dan is still there, serving as the senior pastor of The Lighthouse Church of All Nations, in Alsip, Illinois. Never wavering, he took that small ministry of sixteen people and nurtured it into the largest multicultural church on the south side of Chicago, consisting of more than five thousand members. The driving force of Dan's ministry has always been uniting the races. To look out over the congregation during a typical worship celebration, you will see men, women, and children from over seventy-two different nations.

Confronting the walls of racism and prejudice is never easy, but praise has always been his weapon. Dan is a gifted singer, musician, and producer. He founded a community choir called The Pentecostals of Chicago, a groundbreaking move in 1990, bringing together black, white, Hispanic, and Asian singers from more than twenty Chicago-area churches. This group, now known as The All Nations Choir, has six albums to its credit and has performed with artists from Celine Dion to Kirk Franklin, and on missionary trips to the orphanages of Kingston, Jamaica. Pastor Dan also has two solo albums, the latest being *A Man, His Piano, and His Worship*, a collection of hymns and worship songs.

A celebrated television host, he created and hosted the Emmy Award-nominated *Inspiration Sensation* and *I'm Just Sayin'.* He has traveled the country ministering and teaching men and women through Operation Starting Line, a program of Prison Fellowship, and has also been a national and international speaker on the topics of music, ministry, racial reconciliation, leadership, and community development.

Dan's previous books with Whitaker House include *Freedom to Forget: Releasing the Pain from the Past, Embracing the Hope for the Future* and *Praise is My Weapon*. He and his wife, Linda, are the proud parents of four grown children and eight grandchildren.